Just Shy of Stars

Poems by Annette Hope Billings

Kansas City   Spartan Press   Missouri

Spartan Press
Kansas City, Missouri
spartanpresskc.com

Copyright (c) Annette Hope Billings 2017
First Edition 1 3 5 7 9 10 8 6 4 2
ISBN: 978-1-946642-34-9
LCCN: 2017959796

Design, edits and layout: Jason Ryberg
Author photo: Karen Ledford
Cover image and design: Mallory Goeke
All rights reserved. No part of this publication may be reproduced or transmitted in any form or by any means, electronic or mechanical, including photocopying, recording or by info retrieval system, without prior written permission from the author.

Spartan Press would like to thank Prospero's Books, The Fellowship of N-finite Jest, The Prospero Institute of Disquieted P/o/e/t/i/c/s, Will Leathem, Tom Wayne, Jeanette Powers, j.d.tulloch, Jason Preu, Mark McClane, Tony Hayden and the whole Osage Arts Community.

"Cinqains" was first published in *Valley Falls Vindicator/Homewords Project*/Kansas Humanities Council 1/23/15

CONTENTS

A Case for Poetry / 1

High Shine / 2

One or Two / 3

Well and Good / 4

Rightly Wed / 6

Stay this Course / 8

All Write / 9

Nightshift / 10

The First of Many Cuts / 11

First Right of Refusal / 12

That Settles It / 14

Now What? / 15

Spill / 16

Endless / 18

Just Shy of Stars / 20

Black Girls, Gone / 22

Haiku / 23

Cinqains / 25

Blueberry / 26

Infinite Hallelujahs / 28

The Difference / 30

Time Management / 31

Dayanu / 32

Advanced Directives / 33

Remedy / 34

Director's Notes / 35

Endearments / 36

Journey's End / 37

Rise / 38

First Light / 40

New Math / 41

Soaked / 42

Coral Hibiscus of July / 43

Watch / 44

Molten / 45

Stillborn / 46

Here / 47

Feast / 48

Woman Well / 49

Sentencing / 50

Rampion / 51

Diamonds / 53

The Curious Case of Birthday Carolyn / 55

I'm Okay with Old / 56

Holy Water / 58

There / 60

Old Souls / 61

More Beauty Than Use / 62

In memory of Jessica Elise *Jess* Barron, poet
and person extraordinaire who left this earth far too
soon, but not before she could transform us all
with her words, her fire, and her love.

A Case for Poetry

Poetry requests such brief moments of time,
what it takes to cook a 3-minute egg,
to sew on a button or repot a small plant
with no demands for commitment like novels.

A poem presents itself like a blind date
putting forth its best first impression
flirting and revealing enough of itself
to make you want to read it again.

A poem is content to inhabit meager space,
still it knows it can cover vast ground
and few poems have ever justly been deemed
worth less than the time spent to read them.

High Shine

I pledge to write, with intention, without rest,
words which gleam too many carats to count
and hold too much substance to weigh.
Then I will stand squarely before you
flat-footed, spine straight
to recite some provocative poems
over time, under pressure
in the way coal addresses diamonds
to remind, incite you, inspire you
to write, read, sing, dance, paint
to make some art of your own.

To that end I will nag, harangue, and pester
the latent artist inside of you
until you feel you've no choice
but to come from your closet
and buff your own art to high-shine.

One or Two

It may be no huge crowds will ever await you
and the only *masses* gathered to hear you
will be paltry souls—one or two,
a couplet of poetry patrons
who've heard you might speak a good word.

Still, promise you will, for those sparse listeners,
read for them like they numbered legion
with zest normally reserved for standing room only.
Say you will cherish their quiet applause
like it came from a sold out crowd
and thank them for coming like
they were an audience of enormity.

Do this and know your acclaim may not be
that you drew in hordes of people,
it may be that you shared words with a few
like they were a crowd of many.

Well and Good

It was all well, all entirely good
when they wrote of kittens and flowers
they were fervently greeted
with a cacophony of *oohs,*
and an appreciative avalanche of *ahs*
and as long as their poems weren't contentious
they were held in highest regard.

When the time came for their poetry
to be of injustice and inequality
you sang an entirely different tune
you took it up an entire octave
added more sharps, removed some flats.

Now you find the fruits of their labor too ripe
to the point they draw bile from your gut
you have demoted each one from favored poet
to persona non grata overnight.

But, sometimes a poem is supposed to be
a rock in the heel of your shoe
a lash that falls into the whites of your eye,
a thorn with its home in your side,
a Charley Horse galloping in at 3 am.
They will not always deliver pretty poems,
that was never their intended goal.

Cut their mics if you must,
shred their manuscripts;
there'll be more words in the poets
they will be obliged to write.

Precious kittens, pretty flowers
are scarcely in need of poems
while hard truths plead for verse
so much that what a poet may need to write
is less a sonnet and more a rant.

Rightly Wed
Inspired by William Stafford's

When I Met My Muse

~I glanced at her and took my glasses
off--they were still singing. They buzzed
like a locust on the coffee table and then
ceased. Her voice belled forth, and the
sunlight bent. I felt the ceiling arch, and
knew that nails up there took a new grip
on whatever they touched. "I am your own
way of looking at things," she said. "When
you allow me to live with you, every
glance at the world around you will be
a sort of salvation." And I took her hand.
—William Stafford

I lived with my muse for decades,
an agreement that eschewed
the trappings of traditional matrimony.
We accepted I was the promised bride
in an arranged marriage to nursing
where nightingales sang my praise.

But the day I tendered my resignation,
I danced my muse through corridors
with hands clasped in poetic relief
we made our way to the hospital chapel.

There, with William Stafford's ghost officiating,
we plighted our troths.
Both tearing up
at *until death do us part,*
we exchanged plain gold rings
and left rightly wed.

In these years of writing since
we retain newly wed status—
she still makes me blush
at her nightly, warm and red under brown—
I, Muse, take you, Annette.

Stay this Course

Stay the course—
the artistic path of dubious wisdom,
this convoluted maze of creative uncertainty.
Don blinders if they are required
to keep the practical from distracting you
from the sole thing you may be certain of—
your joy in the making of art.

Exercise more faith than is reasonable,
entertain little doubt as possible,
throw a party for naysaying haters
and set each against another.

If you harbor untold anxiety
about the validity of your choices,
don't stop designing to feed your fear
worry in constant pursuit of your passion.

Even if you question every day
if what you produce earns a label of craft,
trust the answer will be clearly seen
in the bounty of art you create.

All Write

She was calm, so confident
until writing cramps began;
they occurred politely spaced
since it was still early labor.
But when the contractions quickened
and poems stacked one atop the other,
she grew frantic and unsure.
She fretted she had neither strength
nor talent to deliver another poem well.
She feared what she would push to paper
would be judged as premature.

She howled when she broached transition
and clawed at the keyboard in despair.
I can't do this, she moaned to her muse
who sat smiling at her side.
But you are doing it, her muse cooed
*I see the top of this poem's head,
it is ready and you are all write.*

Nightshift

My muses implore me to stay awake
long past what is thought to be wise,
hours after you-should-be-asleep o'clock.
They promise to make a poet of me
if I will only make poems with them.
They buzz at my ears like worrisome gnats,
bothering well into the dark meat of night.
When I dare doze, they tug the hem of my garment
and ply me with propositions of plump verse.
Each muse raises a hand
like a well-fed school child,
Ooooh, pick me, pick me, since you're fully awake.
and we will write away until dawn.
In the morning, I rise poorly-rested,
I splash my face, hoist my pick axe
and coax my weary mind (and my nose)
back to the grindstone.
My solace is the rest I paid for my art
could not have been better spent.

The First of Many Cuts

Words queued up inside me
like jets on a runway
headed for the Hudson,
headed for the flock of geese
called my next attempt to write.

Poems laying transverse in my belly
refuse to rotate head down,
their only exit—
a clean slice across the belly.

Pen poised,
I steady my hand
for the first of many cuts.

First Right of Refusal

I will not do it—
speak some namby-pamby
sentimental bit of verse
after I've seen the women dancing!

I will not do it—
stand and recite pretty prose
when from the corner of my eye
I clearly spy the dip of a hip
the nerve of a curve
and a belly swell of movement.

I will not do it—
deliver some constrained verse
after I've seen how they undulate,
how they captivate
how the motivate the eye
to watch navels and baubles
tassels that reflect the light.

I will not do it—
however I will testify
how they glorify
the joy of dance,

how they ease a sigh
of appreciative breath
from those who know beauty
when it swirls before you.

So I will not do it—
perform some polite little rhyme
of the acceptable kind
now that I've seen the women dancing!

That Settles It

She took the book
fractured its spine
broke its back and
labeled it *mine*
she cracked it so it had to stay
in a place where she could read it all day
in time when the paper began to age
her DNA remained on each page
all it took was one quick look
to know she was a writer
because she had a book.

Now What?

Hate has flung open its gaping maw
to ingest political rhetoric by shovelfuls
not stopping to taste or chew
what began as our amusement.

Sound bytes, formerly just irritating,
have festered and broadcast their true selves
on channels turned too late to stop pus
from pouring what once was the nation's integrity.

Beyond infected,
we are grossly abscessed,
run through with widespread intolerance,
edematous with pockets of division.

Words, once thought rude but harmless,
have morphed into intentional ill will
right in front of our somnolent eyes
and we wonder why contempt spews so freely
from the exact platform we allowed it to build?

To label 45 entertainment
was an irresponsible misnomer
and not a synonym for the
bully he has always been.
Now what?

Spill

My near-perfect carry technique
results in safe transport of coffee
from kind barista to hard table,
no slosh as hot liquid sways
in tandem with my gait.
I have mastered strategy of—
Don't look at it and it won't spill.

I slowly slide the saucer-cup ensemble
onto the table's solid surface,
I edge into the seat and smile at
every drop safe within mug walls.

The black ink on the morning paper
details the latest senseless violence—
the most recent city where blood
flowed from arteries to exsanguination.

Tears still well up,
my vision still blurs
as I read the names of victims
printed neatly below their unsuspecting
smiling pre-mortem photographs.

I avert my eyes from the
bleak news back to my coffee,
sad to find it cooled to tepid.
I ease my cup and newspaper away.

Would that what is true for coffee
were also true for blood—
Don't look at it and it won't spill.

Endless

Before my beautiful brown son left me that night,
I drew him to me
enfolding him against my breasts.
He pulled away in mock disapproval
while I tried to plant endless
kisses on his grinning face.
He tried to wipe every place my lips landed,
so in return I kissed him all the more.
I spanked his bottom like he was still five,
and reminded him mothers always
kiss their children
like each kiss could be the last.
He countered I'd live to kiss him until
I was well past one hundred
and old enough to be *abuela* many times.

I slipped a folded twenty and three condoms
in the back pocket of his jeans.
He reached back and laughed at me.
I sternly made him swear to use them.
He joked he'd certainly spend my money.

He grabbed me and we danced the room,
a Miami salsa, which I matched him step for step.
Be careful tonight, Mijo, I whispered.
His reply, *Me, Mama? Siempre.*

He strode, so handsome, out into evening air
then turned back to say he'd had a chill.
Someone had just walked across his grave.

Hours later my phone startled me awake, an odd call.
My son's furtive voice rasped, *Mama!*
Did I hear fireworks in the background,
then silence as the line went dead?

A short drive to The Pulse Nightclub
and I arrived well before any sirens;
a bloody mayhem met me there,
lifeless bodies being ferried outside,
then the sight of a profile
I knew better than my own
and I wailed to see that slain son was mine.

I fought paramedics as they arrived
and tried to take him from me
like I battled newborn nursery staff
the miraculous night he was born.
My son was dead.
There was no treatment
better than his mother's loving arms.

Before my beautiful brown son left me that night,
I drew him to me enfolding him against my breasts.
He lay quietly, lifeless against me
I planted endless kisses
on his still warm sweet face
like those kisses would be my last.

Just Shy of Stars

A brown girl wanders amber waves;
a gold garland of woven wheat
crowns her head of defiant curls.
Chest tight with longing,
she scours fields for any of Kansas
that bears likeness to her.

Serenaded by meadowlarks,
she kneels to smell rich county soil,
brushing the ground
with her Cupid's bow mouth,
lips lush in a way
that makes the earth feel blessed.

She creeps up near a bison herd,
grins at their hides of richest brown.
They scatter with her cries of
Hey you beauties, dark like me!

A cottonwood invites her to its shade
where she lingers under summer leaves.
She stretches out and is lulled to sleep
by the lilt of honeybee buzz.

She dreams of future difficulties,
of places where she'll find
herself still just shy of stars.
Foreshadowed failures
work to startle her awake
to survey the surrounding land.

She plots a hearty stew of poems
to put meat on her Midwest bones:
its broth rendered thick
and smooth with a roux
of Gwendolyn Brooks and Langston Hughes,
of Aaron Douglas and Gordon Parks
—a stew seasoned to withstand rejection,
a plains meal to leave
her hopeful and uppity enough
to demand her hometown be more than
a good place to dig potatoes—
it must be a good place to grow
black girls too.

Black Girls, Gone

Black girls, gone
in an onyx moment of concussion;
one bomb deftly exploded four lives
with the destructive breath of feral hate.
It snuffed out promising candles,
innocent wicks just barely burned—
Cynthia, Carole, Addie Mae, Denise,
songs extinguished, whole verses unsung,
steps and turns left undanced,

poems they may have written,
shredded and reduced to dusty debris,
stanzas cracked like eggs against a church wall,
seeds of all babies they were to mother
ripped violently out of sweet suspension.

The force of impact still rocks us,
throws us off balance these many years later.
We still suffer the loss, no less profound
and not eased by passing time,
of all gifts they would have offered
to a world so in need of them.
Black girls, gone.

Haiku

1.   Belly full of light
sun surrendered claim on day
fully sated sets.

2.   Always stand regal
whether wearing crown or not;
know you are a queen.

3.   They have come for us
Tiki torches proudly lit
this time without hoods.

4.   April skies sob rain
to save poets from weeping
ink in lieu of tears.

5.   Barometer makes
crank calls of increased pressure.
Joints answer with pain.

6.   Blatant red berries
plump in wintry sparsity:
life among stark death.

7.   Skin to unclothed skin,
a nest of sleeping lovers,
scarcely air between.

8.   Deserted ballroom;
absence makes for sad dancing,
steps for only one.

Cinqains

1. Spent heart
rests in repose
steels itself against break
awaits permission to contract
and fails.

2. Body
tired beyond
all measure of fatigue
calls out for rest that will not come
in time.

3. Head bowed
as though in prayer
is more likely weighed down
with cares more dense than holy words
can lift.

4. This life
temporary
loan of a holding place
where souls linger for a short time
then leave.

Blueberry

She settles in ceramic bowl
awash in deep color,
skin pressed against glazed sides of dish.
She waits there,
filled past full with succulence,
ready to split open, to spill
with slightest provocation,
to darken the fingers,
color the mouths
of we who adore dark berries.

Content to be near midnight blue,
she considers herself radiant
as if she were a hue
to which a blatant red would bow.

Not inclined to sweetness,
she glories in being a little tart,
and only when she fancies,
does she consent to be plucked,
juiced, blended or crushed
to allow her color to be spread.

She presents to me in indigo orbs,
come together to sate my desire
and while worried hordes
in crisp business whites,
give her careful, wide berth,
I scoop her up in glad handfuls,
eager to be deliciously stained.

Infinite Hallelujahs

One day we heard that dreaded word
that stunned the hearts of all who heard:
a diagnosis all have come to fear.
Her doctor called to say the test
revealed a cancer in her breast
that could steal her life and take her *Hallelujah*.
Hallelujah, Hallelujah.

It led us to such deep despair,
it took her breast it took her hair,
it raged ahead despite her valiant fight,
but though her lovely spirit slowed,
cancer could not dull the grace she showed
or phase the beauty of her *Hallelujah*.
Hallelujah, Hallelujah.

In the end, despite her fight,
the thief of cancer took her life
too soon for us to know which way to mourn.
But though her time came to an end
no cancer cell could claim a win
because she left us with her *Hallelujah*.
Hallelujah, Hallelujah

Cancer takes so many lives,
mothers, sisters, daughter and wives,
husbands, brothers, sons are taken too.
Our memories ease the grief of it
and we must vow to never quit,
to breathe and love and live their *Hallelujahs*.
Hallelujah, Hallelujah…

*-In Memory of Susie Perry Copeland, Michelle Lee "Michy" Tizzard
and Clara "Mama" Simmons*

The Difference

Happiness is a babbling brook
coursing giddily in the sun,
always at the mercy of rain,
subject to the whim of a drought.

Joy is an opulent ocean,
immense in depth and width,
not at the mercy of circumstance,
constant in both scarcity and wealth.

Happiness is a handful of kindling:
joy, a sizable log of birch.
No one should trade an ounce of joy
for a pound of happiness
because happiness ignites quickly,
but joy burns long.

Time Management

I spent a good part of yesterday
idly sitting in afternoon sun
beaming in an azure Kansas sky
while a plethora of productive tasks,
which might have been done, was not.
But today's spreading of drizzly gray
casts a malevolent gloom,
which assures me I did not waste yesterday's hours.
It was time wisely spent.

*Dayanu

If I have lived my entire life
just to arrive at this place,
seated, at peace, and grateful
while an October Kansas sun
beats fiercely through a west window,
landing warm blows
on my bowed welcoming neck.
It travels down until skin of shoulders
grants it permission to stay.
If this moment is what it has all been for,
it has been enough.

-in memory of Sandra Moran
*Dayanu is Hebrew for *It would have been enough.*

Advanced Directives

My Living Will instructs,
should my quality of life be unclear,
they are to part my lips,
press a slice of fresh
mango to my mouth,
if I do not stir,
let me go.

Remedy

I lay on Big Mom's plastic covered couch,
head in her lap and my tears on her smock.
I am half past serious heartsick
headed into near critical range.
She pats my back and coos comfort,
tells me I've come just in time.
Had I delayed she might not could have helped me.
My heart would have been beyond repair.
I have neither eaten nor drank for days.
Still, I resist her attempts to nourish me,
but I am weak, she oak tree strong,
and I swallow, as she strokes my throat,
dark liquid she transfers on a spoon.
As I sip her mysterious remedy,
I feel my soul fall open again.
I become rain forest where I'd been desert,
saturated where I was parched.
I feel fertile moving in where barren had been
and every light restored in my soul.
I try to sit up to see the kind of vessel
she has drawn her elixir from
but she moves all her things out of my sight,
says I'll learn to concoct my own.
For now she tells me, *I will un-break your heart,
drink as if tomorrow will not come.*

Director's Notes

    Scene I
Never try to capture grief;
it is feral and cannot be tamed.
Don't design a dam for the tsunami of it,
let it plow through fences as it will
and trample newly laid sod.

    Scene II
Allow grief to howl,
let it bellow and moan.
Don't interrupt its long, sad solo
for which it requests no applause;
it wants only to be fully heard.
Then it will saunter from the spotlight.

    Scene III
Give grief a wide and generous berth
until it allows the return of joy.
After the helter-skelter-to-and-fro of it,
grief will find a quiet alcove of your life
and relinquish center stage.

    Curtain

Endearments

Honey: a syrup-covered term of tenderness.
Sweetheart: a caramel-coated nougat noun.
Sugar: a granulated phrase of fervent fondness.
Sweetiepie: a compound case of pastry passion.
What to make of such sweet terms of endearments,
near obscene in decadence,
these cream-filled phrases of affection,
saccharine sentences spoken like sonnets,
Hershey's Kisses blown across a room,
each delivered Nestle Quick?
The captives of romance gobble them gladly,
beguiled by either love or glucose.

Journey's End

For the wedding of Celeste Hund and Ali Pontius

There is a place in treks of heart
after many relationship miles trod,
a grove of safety appears,
a sanguine sanctuary of utter trust,
which shows itself to be
the home of love's deep longing.

A heart can not help but sigh there and rest,
realizing it has entered a glen
where painful steps of wandering are done
and the time of lonely travels can cease.

This place will be neither stopover,
nor temporary lodge
one might be asked to leave.
It will be an at-long-last destination,
set in a meadow of permanence.
It will be hallowed ground to road weary souls,
a well-deserved and welcome journey's end.

Rise

As night recedes
and dawn ascends,
there lives a moment
when I, night, and she, day, intersect,
where we hang in combined air,
and become entirely each other's.

In this juncture
where ebony and light coincide,
my soul takes deep inspirations
of satin contentment,
exhales sighs of velvet gratitude.

In that shared early space,
my heart leans in,
finds its increase,
commences a sacred glow.

Sunrise unfolds, floods me with
the delivery of promised light,
assures of many radiant occasions
wrapped in a sunlit future.

Ever a gentlewoman,
morning arcs toward me.
I meet her halfway
to offer up my moon-laden heart.

I cling as she mounts sky,
shines herself to full height
and becomes a Kansas horizon.
Within this birth of morning,
I curtsy and fully surrender my dark.
With her new day breath on my skin,
a slow heat penetrates me
until I acquiesce, completely rise too.
We swirl upward,
backlit, blended opposites;
then in unison, across the early sky,
we bear down and deliver day.

First Light

Rise elegantly each morning—
deliberately beautiful,
intentionally new.
Announce yourself with fanfare
and claim each day as your debut.
Challenge everything
that dares try to dull your shine.
No need to wait
for some external sunrise,
be your own.

New Math

She concedes the numbers don't add up,
but according to her lips it feels like
they have not been rightly kissed
for twenty-seven-far-too-many years.
Her lips know what it is to be
both undone and reassembled
by the meeting of mouths.
She can not exactly say how that happens
but if you press your lips to hers
she can show you better than she can explain.

Soaked

I was reminded of you,
of how you open
unafraid of downpours,
of how rain amplifies
your beauty
as you allow your petals
to wear gowns of water
until both of us are soaked.

You are a degree of beauty
that calls for nothing less
than to be showered with kisses,
be those kisses rain
or my lips.

Coral Hibiscus of July

Coral hibiscus of July
opens lovely enough to stop
the most hurried in their tracks.
In response to appreciative sighs
of transfixed onlookers,
it nods,
blooms again.

Watch

I stand on the shoreline,
watch her bathe
and imagine I am that ocean
rising, swelling in foam-capped waves
to dampen her hair,
and rinse her sepia skin.
She will want nothing more
than to wade into the deep of me
where I would coat her
with adoration and salt.

Molten

I want to love you
like the hottest part of fire,
the blue center of flame.
I want to perfect the burn
while crowds gather
to warm their hands over us
as Eros and Cupid egg us on.
We continue until
we are molten.

Stillborn

In the multitude of complex things
that can go awry in pregnancy,
it is a wonder of wonders
most proceed to term.
Can the same be said of romance
when a judge decrees
all our *I love yous* and *I'm sorrys*
must be inventoried and split equally between us?
The truth is we tried hard,
we gave it the best of our best
but in the end we wound up
stillborn.

Here

The end of a relationship
is a first cousin to death
and we find ourselves teetering
on the edge of the fresh grave
where *we're a couple*
has just been laid to rest.
We peer in to do a final search
for the rest of ourselves
in the debris of *us* trapped
in a queue of love's casualties.

We hear reality call our name
grief-stricken, we rasp, *Here.*

Feast

She is a feast of a woman
and those who choose
to only eat salad
will miss more of her
than they will ever know.

She pays no mind
and has little time
for those who come for her
carrying tiny plates.

Her time, far too golden,
her fruit, too abundant
for those who are foreigners
to the beauty in bounty—
those unfortunate souls
who speak with such pride
of their notable passion for nibbling;
she pitys those poor souls
because she is a feast.

Woman Well

Many exalt scarcely-tested youth
with its everything still taut, smooth,
but scant praise is heard for older women
roots deep, branches spread in power:
a woman who is a time-proven wonder
and decades from sapling status
who boasts a lush expanse of confidence,
a solid history of resilience,
and grand display of tensile strength.

Nod your head in appreciation
when you pass by where she stands,
give her foliage your full attention,
tip your hat and stand up straight,
notice leaves cascading from her
scattering wisdom in their wake.
Like a tree who has weathered many seasons,
she has aged to do *older woman* well—
still shelter, still fruit, still shade.

Rampion

Enjoined to remain prisoner,
she grows weary of the wait,
vacates the tower of disparity,
slaying captivity on her own accord.

She exits solitary window,
descends ladder carefully built
with sparse scraps of defiant cypress
and sepia strands of lover's silk.

Her footfalls land brazen
as she clambers steep decline,
leaving a fine residue of victory
upon each succumbing rung.

Crowned by tresses grown for self-delight,
mystical cacophony of lush strands,
coiffed for no one's pleasure but hers,
each hair lies simply at its roots,
then cascades to intentional disarray.

She alights on *terra firma*,
settles at long last on holy ground,
debuts on new-found legs,
ecstatic to bear her full weight at last.

She is a study of acute angles,
sharpness subdued by sugared softness of smile.
She holds back the all-out grin,
coalesced beneath her breasts,
lest she disclose her profound resolve.

All heaven rests in the supra-sternal notch
of skin the hue of peached cream,
and, on telltale tip of artist's brush,
she catches full sight of how fair she is.

This truth, accepted as gospel
as each scripture of oil dries,
proclaims, *No amount of tower time
can dull a destined shine!*

She remains there— transformed,
a rare rampion of enchanted gardens,
content to tarry in paint.

She flushes then smiles once more,
lifts her hem to start her trek
replete in translucent armor
of a woman rescuing herself.

*Written in response to artist Barbara Waterman-Peters' painting
"Rapunzel"*

Sentencing

This is your list of supposed crimes?
These are the things that brought you here?
That you held fast to hope
to a point far beyond reason,
you refused to let surrender be an option,
you persevered despite the gender yoke
they suspended from your neck?
That you hammered away at every *You can't*
until you chiseled each into *Yes, I can!*

Does this represent all offenses
on which your charges were filed?
Then, I'm afraid you leave me no choice;
Woman. I. Pardon. You.

Diamonds

Single mother awake in the night
bends her head over piles of bills
doing her best all by herself
what would be difficult for two.
All demands on her are doubled,
all the resources are halved,
she is the bridge who spans the distance
between ends that never meet.
She is expected to be the answer
for every question asked
which makes her a kind of tired
no amount of rest can resolve.

She makes impossible choices—
pay the light bill or buy shoes?
Always up before sun and her children
so she can weep before they rise.
She could fashion a stew from worry
if it meant her children would eat well.

She stands from the table, wipes her eyes,
dons a smile to awaken the children.
All life has ever issued her has been coal
but it is diamonds she will raise.

The Curious Case of Birthday Carolyn

For the occasion of Carolyn Litwin's 82nd birthday

Sometimes aging must begrudgingly acquiesce
to the vibrancy of a strong woman
who declines to stand idly by
and let a mere 8 and 2/10 decades
steal her unabashed vigor.

Time passes for her, but it grows weary
of trying to do what time does.
It throws up hands in desperation
and pouts its way off to those
more amenable to getting old.

Age can't diminish those it can't catch—
what with tennis lessons
and coordinating gardens,
the designing of florals
and playing of Mahjong!

Nary a hint of senescence
in the poems she authors,
no dulling of her keen appreciation
for all things and all people artistic.

Yes, she is solidly in her winter
but, oh my, how she still blooms!
She is elderly clearly only in years
and though there is more time
behind than before her,
she remains a deep well of curiosity,
a veritable ocean of energy,
aware and appreciative of the gift of each day.

And if time happens to come up even with her,
she will glance at it sideways and sternly
tell it to politely wait its turn
and dare it to hurry her.

So, BabyBoomers and Millennials,
Gen- Xers and Generation Y,
pay close attention and take good notes—
if you're going to live long, live well,
make every day your best day
and declare *every* age to be your prime!

I'm Okay with Old

I hold no animosity
toward my many varicosities,
I'm okay with greying hair
and boring white underwear.
I'm okay with old, I'm okay with old.

I'm have my share of aching joints
and bosoms which no longer make their point,
I'm not sure just what went wrong,
they once were big, now they're just long.
I'm okay with old, I'm okay with old.

As for chins I have a few
but what's a well fed gal to do,
I understand that in the *end*
fiber truly is my friend.
I'm okay with old, I'm okay with old.

I embrace my puffy eyes
and my chubby cellulitic thighs,
I don't much mind my baggy skin
because I love the dame within.
I'm okay with old, I'm okay with old.

I've given in to all my wrinkles
and how often I have to tinkle,
I'm good with wiggly upper arms
cause I've held fast to all my charms.
I'm okay with old, I'm okay with old.

It's true I have two knees that creak
but I can still make suitors weak,
It may take me a longer while
but when I step, I still step with style.
I'm okay with old, I'm okay with old

I don't care what youth has got,
I still have gems which youth does not.
I'm okay with old!

Holy Water

I, Water,
having fully drenched each part you present,
find you faultless.
I find you totally acceptable,
utterly free of error,
and entirely worthy
to enter deep into me.

I, Water,
part for your descent,
yield for your departure.
I covet the sum of you,
caress the all of you,
welcome the whole of you
which you so generously bring.

I, Water,
feel no excess
in wake of your body's passing.
I swirl around you,
ripple against you,
flow beside you,
lap between you.

I, Water,

find you exuberantly sufficient, clothed or naked,

to step, wade, float, tread, splash, spin, stroke as you will,

while you want,

until, saturated with me,

you fancy to exit.

I, Water,

having shamelessly soddened

your every surface,

deem you perfect,

and I bless you for your presence

which renders me holy.

There

At the place where she realizes she is finite,
where she can admit to her insurmountable limits
and can only do so precious much,
where she comes across walls
no one person is expected breach unaided.
Right there.

Right there, she takes certain comfort,
and surrenders to the knowledge
she was never the correct place
for humanity to forward its struggles.

Right there, she rubs her shoulders
in gratitude for their broadness,
the unarguable strength in their span.
But now she understands the truth;
they are merely shoulders,
not steel columns or earth movers
and certainly not load-bearing beams
to carry the weight of the world.

Old Souls

Those who were made
old souls by the horrors
of their childhood know
life can be lived
well in reverse,
so they are delighted
but not surprised
to have dreams
inconsistent with their age.

More Beauty Than Use

She will likely tire
of butterflies as she ages
and turn her affection and energy
to important things of greater weight.
Who's ever seen an old woman
content to sit and grin
at things of far more beauty than use?

Annette Hope Billings is an award-winning poet and actress from the Midwest. Her dynamic style of reciting has led fans to dub her "the Maya of the Midwest." Her first book of poetry, *A Net Full of Hope* (2015), garnered the 2015 ARTSConnect ARTY Award in Literature. Her next book, *Descants for a Daughter* (2016), was a collection of affirmations. Her poetry can also appears in the following anthologies: *Gimme Your Lunch Money: Heart land Poets Respond to Bullying* (2016), *Twisting Topeka* (2016), *Our Last Walk: Using Poetry for Grieving and Remembering Our Pets*.(2016), and *Kansas Time + Place: An Anthology of Heartland Poetry* (Balkans Press, 2017). Billings' poetry can also be found in both online and print publications including *Coal City Press* (2016) and *Konza Magazine* (2016 and 2017). To view short videos of her poetry performances, visit tinyurl.com/anfohvideos, her website at http://anetfullofhope.com /, her facebook: anetfullofhope, or on Twitter: @AnnetteBilling3

www.ingramcontent.com/pod-product-compliance
Lightning Source LLC
Chambersburg PA
CBHW021450080526
44588CB00009B/782